CREEPY, KOOKY SCIENCE

Bizarro Bloodsuckers

Ron Knapp

Enslow Publishing
101 W. 23rd Street
Suite 240
New York, NY 10011
USA

enslow.com

Published in 2019 by Enslow Publishing, LLC.
101 W. 23rd Street, Suite 240, New York, NY 10011

Library of Congress Cataloging-in-Publication Data

Names: Knapp, Ron, author.
Title: Bizarro bloodsuckers / Ron Knapp.
Description: New York : Enslow Publishing, 2019. | Series: Creepy, kooky
science | Audience: Grades 5-8. | Includes bibliographical references and index.
Identifiers: LCCN 2018010347| ISBN 9781978503731 (library bound) | ISBN
9781978505483 (pbk.)
Subjects: LCSH: Bloodsucking animals—Juvenile literature.
Classification: LCC QL756.55 .K5824 2019 | DDC 591.5/3—dc23
LC record available at https://lccn.loc.gov/2018010347

Printed in the United States of America

To Our Readers: We have done our best to make sure all websites in this book were active and appropriate when we went to press. However, the author and the publisher have no control over and assume no liability for the material available on those websites or on any websites they may link to. Any comments or suggestions can be sent by email to customerservice@enslow.com.

Portions of this book originally appeared in *Bloodsucking Creatures*.

Contents

Introduction

Humans and other mammals need blood. It delivers proteins, oxygen, and sugars to all parts of our bodies. Even while you sleep, your heart keeps you alive by pumping blood through your arteries and veins.

When you get a cut, blood leaks out. But if it's not a large wound, the leaking soon stops. Tiny disks called platelets plug up the hole. The blood at the wound thickens into something like jelly. This thickening is called coagulation. Soon the thick blood dries and turns into a scab. No more leaking. Slowly the skin grows back together. The wound is healed.

Bloodsuckers are animals that want our blood. They suck it out of our bodies—usually without us noticing. Not even coagulation can stop them. You might think that thick blood would be impossible to suck. But the bodies of bloodsuckers produce anticoagulants that stop the blood from thickening.

Bloodsuckers are usually small animals who have scary-looking mouths. Some of them have triple jaws or tongues covered with teeth. But they do their work quietly and carefully. It's possible right now that tiny mosquitoes or fleas or lice are sucking your blood . . . and you don't even know it.

Gobs of platelets (light brown) flow through the bloodstream along with red blood cells.

Don't worry. These bloodsuckers are not going to steal all your blood. You won't even miss the little bit they take. Mostly they just irritate us. Have you ever been outside when clouds of mosquitoes are driving you crazy? Has your school ever been hit by an epidemic of head lice? Have you suffered through the special shampoo treatment and stiff painful combs? What about your pets? Have they ever been attacked by fleas?

Sometimes we make jokes about head lice. We love silly, scary stories about vampire bats. We pretend they turn into humans with tuxedos and big teeth. There have been popular romantic stories about handsome vampires. Maybe you dressed up as Count Dracula for Halloween.

Some people like bloodsuckers because they are so gross. What could be more repulsive than a tiny bat sucking blood out of the foot of a sleeping cow? Have you ever scratched an itchy head and wondered if tiny eggs were hatching in your hair? Now that's disgusting.

But sometimes bloodsuckers can be worse than gross. They can be killers. One of the most dangerous creatures of all time is a bloodsucker you could squash with your pinky. The flea has been responsible for the deaths of millions.

Bloodsuckers don't try to be cool or disgusting or dangerous. They're not trying to drive us crazy or make us itch. They're not interested in killing people.

Like other creatures, they just want to live. Sucking blood keeps them alive.

CHAPTER 1

Mosquitoes: Tiny Flying Terrors

They don't look like much. Their name comes from the Spanish words *mosca* plus *ito*, which means "little fly." Mosquitoes are so small and light that it would take three hundred thousand of them to weigh as much as a can of soda. You can walk faster than they can fly. A mosquito lives only two or three weeks.

But for hundreds of thousands of years, these have been very dangerous creatures. For years, they stopped the building of the Panama Canal. Mosquitoes have caused the deaths of millions of people.

The little fly has a skinny body with three parts—a head, thorax, and abdomen. There are three pairs of legs. Sticking out of the head is a long skinny tube called a proboscis. Mosquitoes stay alive by using it to suck nectar out of flowers.

A mosquito inserts its proboscis into human skin and sucks out blood.

When it flies, the female mosquito sounds like a tiny engine. Her wings beat almost five hundred times a second, making a weird buzzing sound. That's her way of getting the attention of the male mosquitoes. They flock around a female as soon as they hear her buzzing. She mates with one, then flies away with the male's sperm stored in her body.

After that, her mate has nothing left to do. Within two weeks, he's dead. The female lives much longer. She has an important job to do. Hundreds of eggs begin to grow inside her body. She needs to nourish them, but nectar won't help. It is mostly made of sugar. The only food that will make the eggs grow properly is animal blood.

Finding Blood

One of the best sources of blood is human beings. Mosquitoes can find you—even in the dark—because their antennae sense the chemicals given off by your body. They drill into your skin and suck out your blood. The proboscis of the female is covered with sharp, jagged stylets. They pump up and down furiously as she jabs her proboscis into your skin. Once inside, she bends it back and forth, looking for a tiny blood tube called a capillary.

When she finds blood with her proboscis, the female pours saliva into your body. It thins your blood so that it is easier for her to suck. Then she pumps the blood through a small tube in her proboscis. It takes only about ninety seconds for her to fill her abdomen with blood. By then she's dark and swollen.

After she is finished, the female pulls her proboscis out of your skin and flies away. For the next few days she rests, allowing her body to digest its bloody meal. The eggs grow, and soon she lays them in water.

Mosquito Bites

But what about you? Usually you do not even notice being bitten. You are so much larger than a mosquito that you don't miss the tiny amount of blood sucked out of your body. What you do notice is the swelling around the bite. The mosquito's saliva irritates your skin.

To fight the irritation, your body produces chemicals called histamines. A small bump forms around the bite. For a while, it itches. Dr. Melissa Piliang, a dermatologist at Cleveland Clinic, recommends putting ice on the bite to relieve the itch.[1]

No Scratching!

Mosquito bites itch, but the worst thing to do is to scratch them. Scratching makes your body release even more histamines, which make the bump even bigger and itchier. Have you ever scratched so hard the bites turned bloody? Your scratching fingernails have ripped open the skin around the bite. The dirt under your nails can get into the wound. Soon you've got a nasty infection. The swelling will get even worse.

If itchy little bumps were the only problems caused by mosquitoes, scientists and doctors would not worry about them.

But sometimes, mosquitoes spread diseases. When a female squirts her saliva into a victim, it can be full of germs taken from a person or an animal bitten a few minutes earlier. The germs get into the new victim's body and can cause serious diseases such as yellow fever, malaria, and encephalitis.

Gorgas Beats the Mosquitoes in Panama

About a hundred years ago, mosquitoes almost prevented the building of the Panama Canal. French companies wanted to dig the canal through the jungles of Panama to connect the Atlantic and Pacific Oceans. It was a hot, swampy area—a perfect spot for mosquitoes to lay their eggs. The female mosquitoes feasted on the blood of thousands of workers. Soon, the workmen began dying from malaria and yellow fever. Finally, the French gave up and went home.

Netting like this helped make the Panama Canal possible. It lets air through but not mosquitoes.

That's when William Gorgas (1854–1920), an American sanitation expert, went to work. He drained swamps around the route of the canal so the mosquitoes would not have a place to lay their eggs. He sprayed oil and insecticides to kill the pesky insects. He put screens on windows and covered beds with mosquito netting. Soon, the workers were safe, and the canal was completed.

The Danger of DDT

Today, modern medicines have just about wiped out most of the diseases carried by mosquitoes in the United States, but the insects are still a nuisance. In the 1940s and 1950s, scientists thought they had the answer: a chemical called DDT, which is an insecticide that kills almost all mosquitoes. Thousands of acres were sprayed. The mosquito problem was almost solved, but a brand-new problem was created when a few of the mosquitoes survived. They were immune to DDT, and the chemical did not bother them at all. The mosquitoes that hatched from their eggs were immune, too. It took stronger and stronger doses of DDT and other poisons to kill them. But those chemicals also killed wildlife and made many people sick. The use of DDT was stopped in the United States in the early 1970s.

Still Fighting Mosquitoes

Today, scientists have many ways to control insects and don't rely solely on insect poisons. They are experimenting with chemical traps that attract mosquitoes but do not bother anything else.[2]

They also use animals such as bats that love to eat mosquitoes. Scientists are looking for species of insects that could eat mosquito larvae and for tiny wasps that eat mosquito eggs.

You, too, can help fight mosquitoes. Make sure your family does not leave standing water around your house. Thousands of eggs can be laid in a soggy ditch or an old barrel filled with water. Spraying mosquito repellent on your skin will not kill the bugs, but it will keep them away from you. The repellent works by preventing mosquitoes from noticing the heat and moisture given off by your body. They cannot "see" you with their antennae, so they leave you alone.

Dozens of tiny mosquito eggs hatch in water.

People used to think that eating bananas or garlic would keep mosquitoes away. Scientists say no way. However, it looks like they are attracted by some perfumes and even the smell of stinky feet.[3]

Researchers believe your clothes make a difference. Mosquitoes are attracted by dark colors, especially if you are moving around. It's harder for them to notice khaki or beige. Try to wear layers of loose clothing. A mosquito proboscis can poke right through a thin tight shirt.

And remember that mosquitoes are most active at dawn and dusk. If the sun is high and hot, they're usually resting.

Trillions and Trillions

It is estimated that there are one hundred trillion mosquitoes in the world today. That is about twenty thousand for every person on the planet. Each day about thirty-three trillion—or one-third—of the mosquitoes die. Some are swatted and squashed by irritated humans, but most are eaten by bats, lizards, birds, and spiders. The mosquitoes are an important part of their diet. If the tiny bloodsucking insects disappeared, the animals that eat them would be in trouble. Luckily for the bats, lizards, birds, and spiders, all the mosquitoes that die are quickly replaced by trillions more that hatch.

Mosquitoes can be controlled but probably never eliminated. After all, they have been around a long, long time. Millions of years before the first humans, they were already here, sucking the blood out of dinosaurs.

CHAPTER 2

Vampire Bats: Preying on Sleeping Victims

Imagine a huge cave in Central or South America. It's hot and sticky. And dark. Very dark. So dark you can't see the thousands of tiny vampire bats hanging from the ceiling.

The bats aren't pretty. They have big ears, claws, and razor-sharp teeth. Their tongues are bright red. Their bodies are reddish-brown. They look like scary mice with long, dark wings.

Vampire bats are amazing creatures. Like other bats, they find their way through the dark by echolocation, a kind of animal radar. They send out tiny sounds that bounce off objects. When the echo hits their ears, they know what's around them.

A vampire bat shows its sharp fangs as it hangs onto a cave wall.

Unlike other bats, vampire bats have powerful legs. They can walk, hop, and even run. They also have tiny thermoreceptors on their noses. Somehow these allow them to "see" the heat given off by animals in the dark. They can probably also spot the warmest area on the bodies of their victims, the parts with the most blood. Scientists are still studying this amazing ability.

The Action Is at Night

Like most other bats, vampire bats are nocturnal, which means they sleep through the day so they can be active at night. Their schedule works out well because they can only get their nourishment when their victims are sleeping. No animal that is awake and alert would let a vampire bat get anywhere near it.

When the sun goes down, the bats get busy. They fly out of their caves looking for a meal. Vampire bats think cattle blood is very tasty. They also like blood from pigs, goats, and birds. Sometimes they will even land on a human and start sucking. They're not fussy. If an animal has blood, it is a possible victim.

Dogs are one of the few types of animals that are not bothered much by vampire bats. That's because dogs hear so well. Vampires make a high-pitched screeching sound when they fly. Dogs hear the noise and wake up. If an animal is awake, the vampire bat will fly right by.

Time for Supper

Once a vampire bat finds a suitable victim, it lands nearby, usually on the ground. Then it tucks its big, thin wings under its body and closes in. Hopping and creeping silently on its clawed feet, the bat looks for the best place to strike. Since the vampire bat is so light, the sleeping victim usually does not even notice the footsteps up its leg or across its back.

A vampire bat quietly sucks the blood of a pig.

Soon, the bat has picked its spot. Its razor-like teeth shave off any hair or fur. Then the triangular teeth sink into the flesh of the victim. On cattle, the neck is the best place to strike. The skin is soft there and filled with veins and arteries. A lot of blood can also be found in the nose of a pig or the ear of a goat. On humans, the best spots are fingers, toes, lips, and the forehead.

No matter the spot, and regardless of the type of animal, the result is the same. Once the teeth are removed from the tiny wound, the victim begins to bleed. The bat's saliva keeps the blood from clotting into a scab. Now it's feeding time!

So that it does not miss a drop, the bat curls its tongue into a funnel. The blood travels through the tongue, into the mouth, down the esophagus, and into the stomach. A vampire bat's digestive system cannot handle solid foods. Blood is the only thing that can keep it alive.

While it's slurping, the bat keeps very quiet and still. It wants its victim to stay asleep so that the meal can continue. After about half an hour of slurping, the vampire bat has to stop. Its stomach is so full, it can barely fly back to its cave. When it finally gets there, it falls asleep and lets its body digest the blood.

Meanwhile, the victim is probably still asleep. Usually, the wound bleeds a little bit after the bat leaves. Human victims might notice a little blood on their bedclothes when they wake up, but they will probably have trouble finding the wound. Vampire bats don't leave much of a trace. Their bite is only about 0.1 inch (0.3 centimeter) wide. You can get much worse cuts from bumping into a door or falling off your bike. Human victims will probably never miss the blood stolen during the night. Since vampire bats are so tiny, birds are usually the only animals they can bleed to death.

Sometimes, a vampire bat cannot find a meal before it returns to its cave. But it doesn't need to go hungry if it has good friends to rely on. Vampire bats can recognize each other and will ask another bat to share its blood meal, which it can regurgitate into its friend's mouth. Next time, their roles may be reversed and the favor is paid back. The bats can remember who shared with them in the past. They are willing to share with the bats that helped them out when they needed it. If a mother bat dies, other females will care for her orphans.[1]

Draculin

Draculin is the anticoagulant found in the saliva of vampire bats. It's named after Count Dracula, the most famous of the fictional human vampires. Draculin stops the victim's blood from clotting. It works so well that scientists are experimenting to see if it could be used as a medicine for humans. People suffering from strokes need to keep their blood flowing freely. Maybe someday they'll take draculin.

Vampires Are Bats, Not People

For humans and most animals, the problem with vampire bats is not the blood they take, but the microorganisms they leave behind. The teeth and saliva of the bats often carry bacteria and viruses that cause dangerous infections. Some of their victims get rabies, a disease that destroys nerve cells in the brain. If left untreated and without proper medication, death will result.

For centuries, people in Europe have told frightening stories about human vampires who must suck the blood of other humans to stay alive. Supposedly, a vampire is very tough to kill—you have to put a stake through its heart. The people of Europe need not worry because, of course, there have never been any human vampires. Today, there are no real vampire bats living there—or in the United States, either. The bats living in Europe and the United States are not interested in blood. Their idea of a good time is a night spent eating insects.

The world's only real bloodsucking bats live in Central and South America and on a few Caribbean islands. Most of the time, they do not bother humans. It's a lot easier to get the blood they need from cattle or other farm animals.

CHAPTER 3

Head Lice: Making a Home in Your Hair

Have you ever had a little cut on your head? Were you surprised by all the blood? That's because your scalp is covered by tiny blood tubes called capillaries. Head lice don't have to work very hard to find plenty of blood.

And what better hiding place than a forest of hair? A louse is about the size of a sesame seed. It's pale, almost transparent. It would be hard to see if it was out in the open.

Lice are just as hard to feel. They don't do much crawling around. Unless somebody looks at your head very carefully, they probably won't spot them. Sometimes a magnifying glass will help.

Chances are you won't suspect you have head lice until you feel what they are doing to your head. By that time, they are warm and comfortable, hanging tightly to your hair, laying eggs, and sucking your blood.

Sharing with Friends

Kids are usually the ones who get head lice. Of course, it's not because they don't keep their hair clean. It's because kids do things that make it easy for a louse or two to make it from one head to another. Have you ever wrestled with a friend? Sat so close to a classmate that your heads were touching? Shared a pillow with a pal at a slumber party? Those are great chances for lice to move.

Claws Grab, Teeth Bite

A louse's body is very simple and efficient. The curved claws on its six legs are designed to grasp hold of hairs so that the insect can have a firm grip while it goes to work. The louse uses tiny teeth to bite into the skin of the scalp. Then it drops a long beak into the fresh wound. Soon, it is sucking blood right out of the victim's head.

The person usually does not feel the louse's bite or the blood being sucked out. The louse is free to drink until it is full. By then, it is no longer pale. Its color is dark red from all the blood it has swallowed.

More and More Lice

One louse will not cause much of a problem, but most people do not have just one louse for long. One female can lay as many as ten eggs a day.[1] She glues her white eggs one at a time to single strands of hair. The eggs, or nits as they are sometimes called, are easier to spot than the lice themselves. They look like dandruff or pieces of light-colored dust, but they cannot be brushed off or blown away like dandruff. They are stuck securely to the hairs.

If the eggs are not removed, they will hatch in about ten days. The new lice lay more eggs. Soon, the

A tiny louse holds tight to strands of human hair.

person's head becomes the home of a community of the pests. They do not suck enough blood to cause the person serious harm, and they do not carry any dangerous diseases, but their bites soon begin to itch. For many people, the first indication of head lice comes when they notice how much they are scratching their heads. The itchiest spots are usually behind the ears and on the back of the head. There, the hair is thickest and the lice have more places to hide.[2]

A special comb is used to scrape the nits off the hair.

A Stubborn Problem

People don't get head lice because their hair is dirty. They get it because their head comes into contact with the head of some-body who already has head lice. A louse can move on over to a new head

Scratching will not get rid of lice. Neither will regular soap or shampoo. A good hard shower might shake loose most or even all of the lice. The problem is the nits are still there. Soon they hatch and you've got a headful of lice again.

The only way to make sure all the lice are gone is to use a special shampoo designed to kill all the lice and the nits. Some doctors also recommend using a special comb that will be sure to remove all the nits from the hair.

However, washing and combing are often not enough, even with special shampoos and combs. Sometimes lice are accidentally knocked off onto combs, brushes, towels, sheets, blankets, or clothing. From there, they can find their way right back onto a head that has just been cleaned. The problem begins all over again. Any household item that came in contact with the hair must be thoroughly cleaned.

It is a lot harder to get rid of lice than it is to stay away from them in the first place. Health officials advise people not to share combs, hats, and scarves. If students are not careful, lice can spread to a whole classroom in just a few weeks. Soon, everybody is itching!

CHAPTER 4

Lampreys: Lurking in the Rivers

ampreys have been around for thousands of years. They are fish, but they have no scales. Their bodies are shaped not by bones, but by soft cartilage. They look more like fat eels or worms than fish. Lampreys range in size from 5 to 40 inches (13 to 102 cm).

A lamprey has seven gills, one nostril, and one eye. Old folk stories called them "nine-eyed eels" because people thought the gills and nostrils were eyes, too.

But what everybody noticed about lampreys were their big mouths. No jaws, just a wide hole at one end. Ancient Romans watched them use those big mouths to anchor themselves to stones at the bottom of streams. They named the blobs "lampreys" or "stone suckers."

Sometimes the weird creatures pull the stones loose and collect piles of them. They travel by sucking onto fish and going for a ride.

Rows of sharp teeth circle the lamprey's mouth.

Hanging on by Sucking

Scientists later figured out that lampreys anchor themselves with their mouths onto big rocks so that they can rest. It's not easy swimming against the current, but that's what they have to do on their way to spawn, or lay eggs. Prior to spawning, the male makes a nest from a pile of little stones.

When the nest is completed, the male uses his sucker to anchor himself to the female. Then he wraps his body around her, squeezing tightly so that thousands of eggs are pushed out of her body. As the eggs fall into the nest, he fertilizes them with his sperm. Soon, both parents are dead, exhausted from the long trip upstream and the laying of the eggs.

Fierce Food

We might think they look gross, but lampreys used to be a popular, high-class food. European kings and queens thought they tasted like meat, not fish. One of the favorite royal dishes was lamprey pie. The wormlike fish were cooked in syrup inside the pie. Then the crust was opened so wine and spices could be poured in. There is a legend that eating too many lampreys killed England's King Henry I in 1135. When Queen Elizabeth II celebrated sixty years on the throne in 2012, the people of Gloucester, England, baked her a lamprey pie.

Growing Slowly in the Sand

When the offspring hatch, they are on their own. At first, they don't look much like their parents. They appear to be tiny, transparent worms. To hide from predators, they burrow into the soft sand of the streambed. Only their big mouths stick out of the sand, catching small organisms. As the lampreys grow, their slimy skin turns tan or brown. They continue to hide in the sand until they're fully grown. Sometimes that takes as long as seven years.

They Don't Let Go

A lamprey is a perfectly designed sucking machine. Its round mouth can easily attach to almost any surface. Lampreys do not just suck stones or hold on to other lampreys. When they are fully grown, they stop eating organisms that happen to swim into their mouths. As adults, they become deadly bloodsuckers.

Their victims are almost always fish. Lampreys rarely attack people. They keep away from the warmth of the human body. That's lucky for us, since these bloodsuckers usually hang on to their victims for long periods of time. Tiny teeth on the inside of the lamprey's mouth dig into the scales of the unlucky fish. They are almost impossible to shake off.

Have you ever heard of a tongue with teeth? That's what does most of the work for the lamprey. Scientists call the extra teeth dental plates. They are so jagged and sharp that the lamprey can open a large wound just by scraping its tongue back and forth. Then the sucking begins. To make the job easier, the lamprey injects a powerful chemical into its victims. Not only does this chemical stop the blood from clotting, but it also dissolves the tissues around the wound.

A lamprey is patient. It will keep sucking for four or five hours. If its victim is a small fish, the lamprey will usually suck it dry, and the animal will not be released until it is dead. On a larger fish or a whale, the lamprey will suck on one spot for a while, then move to another part of the same body. After a while, it moves on to another victim before it has sucked all the blood out of a large animal. That fortunate survivor is easy to spot. For the rest of its life, it will bear a round scar from the attack.

Invasion of the Great Lakes

Even if they do not like the taste of humans, lampreys have caused plenty of other kinds of trouble for them. For centuries, sea

Once it's attached, a lamprey can suck for hours on a fish.

lampreys could not move into the Great Lakes from the Atlantic Ocean because they were stopped by Niagara Falls. Then the Welland Canal and St. Lawrence Seaway were built to connect the Great Lakes to the Atlantic Ocean. Lampreys found they could use the canal as easily as the ships could. Soon, they had made their way into all the Great Lakes, where they feasted on the blood of millions of fish. Many types of fish began to disappear. In a year or so, each lamprey can kill as much as 40 pounds (18 kilograms) of fish.[1] Fishermen feared there would be nothing left in the Great Lakes except lampreys. Miles of nets were strung up to catch the bloodsuckers. Even electric fences were built across streams. Nothing worked until scientists tried a chemical called TFM, which killed lampreys but did not seem to harm any other fish. Soon, the lamprey population in the Great Lakes began to fall.

Fish and wildlife agencies then restocked the lake with trout and coho salmon, a non-native species in the Great Lakes region.

Scientists from the United States and Canada continue to explore new ways to keep lampreys out of the Great Lakes. They've mapped the animal's genome, looking for weaknesses in its DNA.[2] Ideally, researchers would like to convince lampreys to stay away without having to kill them.

Scientists are hoping for a better solution than TFM, which, of course, is a poison. If lampreys can be kept under control, they can serve as food for many larger fish and birds.

CHAPTER 5

Fleas: Spreading Death and Disease

You've probably never worried much about fleas. They're a problem for our pets, not us. We feel bad watching our pets scratch and bite their fur to get rid of the nasty pests. Every year, American dog owners spend $380 million on flea prevention.

But fleas have caused much worse problems than being itchy pets. Seven centuries ago, fleas almost killed all the people in Europe. It was the bubonic plague, or Black Death.

A flea is a very tiny killer, only about 0.125 inch (0.318 cm) long. It's flat and almost transparent. What causes the trouble is its sharp skinny proboscis. Fleas want blood. They don't care if it comes from dogs or cats or people. Or even rats.

A tiny flea rests on a person's skin.

Duing the Middle Ages, every big city in Europe had thousands of big, furry rats. The nasty rodents also lived in the busy ships that traveled from country to country. Fleas love rat blood. Nobody knew it was infected by the Black Death.

A Fine Hairy Home

Rats are a fine home for fleas. Their hairs provide a good place to hide. Since fleas are tiny, flat insects, it is very easy for them to crawl between hairs. They're covered with shiny plates that make them very hard. They're almost impossible to squish. When a flea is hungry, it just sinks its sharp proboscis into the rat's skin. Then the flea sticks a pair of pumping tubes from its mouth into the victim. One sucks up the blood, while the other pumps saliva into the wound. The saliva contains a chemical that prevents clotting. It will also make the wound itch when the flea is done.

Killer Fleas

Fleas became killers by sucking the blood of the plague-infected rats. Eventually, the rats would die, and the fleas would move on to new victims, usually other rats. Even though they do not have wings, fleas have no trouble moving. With their strong hind legs, they can jump as far as 13 inches (33 cm).

The blood of the sick rats infected the fleas, too. The germs in the fleas' blood multiplied quickly in the insects' intestines. Soon, their clogged intestines made it impossible for the fleas to digest any blood.

In a desperate attempt to stay alive, the fleas kept sucking blood from their new victims, but there was no place to put it. The fleas spit up germs into the fresh wound. Soon, the infected fleas were dead. However, they had already passed on the disease. More fleas hatched and took their place.

Sometimes when a rat died, its fleas would move onto the body of a nearby human being. Soon, the person was infected by the vomit of the sick insects. Within a few days, the person

This oil painting by nineteenth-century Italian artist
Baldassarre Calamai depicts the bodies of plague victims
being blessed by a priest in Florence, Italy, in 1348.

had the plague. At first, the person just felt weak and uncomfort-
able. Then parts of his or her body began to swell, and purple
blotches appeared on the skin. The person's heart beat faster and
faster, trying to get blood through the swollen tissues. After about
five days, the pain became very intense. The sufferer began to
scream and beg for mercy. Finally, the person lost control of his or
her muscles and made strange, jerky movements. After that, the
victim of the horrible disease finally died.

The Flea Circus

About two hundred years ago, real fleas would pull miniature carts, turn little Ferris wheels, or move balls. A "ringmaster" would announce the tricks and brag about training the little insects. Of course, the fleas weren't really trained. They were just trying to get out of the tiny harnesses. Their efforts caused the movements. The first flea circuses were designed by watchmakers who wanted to show off their skills building tiny machines. To view the action, audiences needed magnifying glasses.

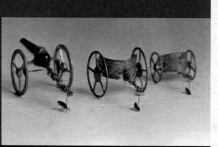

Three flea circus "performers" are attached to tiny chariots.

Soon, the streets were filled with the rotting bodies of plague victims. Everybody was terrified. They wanted to make sure they did not get the disease themselves. But they did not understand how it was spread, so they did some things that seem strange to us. They tried to avoid the plague by smearing their bodies with onions. Maybe the bad smell could keep it away.[1] They blamed people with different religions for bringing the disease into their town, so they burned down their places of worship and killed them. If somebody in a family got the plague, sometimes their home was walled up—with the uninfected members still inside—so that the disease could not "get out." One general turned the plague into a weapon. He put dead, infected bodies on catapults and flung them into his enemy's camps.[2]

Nobody suspected that the cause of all this horror was the pesky little fleas. Back then, the tiny pests were a normal part of everyday life. Everybody had them, since hardly anybody ever took baths and most people did not think of changing clothes. Rich women wore fancy flea traps, but they were not very effective. One of Sweden's queens even tried to get rid of her fleas by shooting them with a tiny crossbow. While they were scratching all their flea bites, nobody in the Middle Ages realized that those tiny insects were killing them.

Still a Problem

Luckily for us, modern cities have gotten rid of millions of rats. There are still plenty of fleas, but they can be controlled by chemicals. Scientists have also developed new medicines that help prevent the plague from breaking out again.

Fleas are not much of a problem in the United States today. We change our clothes regularly, so they can't hide there or lay their eggs in the seams. A good hot shower can usually send most fleas on their way. Probably the most effective weapon against them is the vacuum cleaner. Fleas love to lay eggs in thick, lush carpeting. Vacuum cleaners can easily suck them all up before they hatch.

Today, when we think of fleas, we mostly worry about the pain they cause our pets. Cats and dogs are the main victims now. Even when fleas do not carry dangerous diseases, their bites still itch. Animals scratch very hard to get rid of them. Sometimes they make themselves bleed. Veterinarians recommend sprays, special shampoos, and even flea collars to get rid of the pests. Since they sometimes nest in the area where a pet sleeps, it's also a good idea to change the bedding regularly.

Other parts of the world are not so lucky. In September 1993, an earthquake drove a large population of rats from the jungle near Bid, India. Soon the rats—and their fleas—came in contact with people. Less than a year later, hundreds of the people had the plague.[3] Once again, fleas had transferred the terrible disease from the rats to human beings, and the world was reminded that fleas can be killers.

CHAPTER 6

Leeches: Performing Medical Miracles

n 1799, George Washington had a sore throat. He was sure he knew what was wrong. He had too much blood—or at least too much bad blood. Our first president asked to be "bled." Cuts were made, and about half of his blood was drained out.

The treatment didn't work. Losing all that blood just made him weaker. George Washington was soon dead.

"Doctors" had been bleeding patients for hundreds of years. Soon after Washington's death, they stopped slicing their patients with tools. Bloodsucking little worms called leeches would do the work. Doctors would just place several leeches on the patient's skin. They would drill and start sucking. When the leeches were full, they quit sucking and rolled off.

The three jaws of a leech can cut through a victim's skin.

For a while, leeches were big business. Doctors in France were using forty million a year.

Three Jaws to Do the Drilling

There are many kinds of leeches. They range in length from 0.5 inch (1.3 cm) to almost 12 inches (30.5 cm). Their bodies have two suckers, a big one at the bottom and a smaller one at the head. They use the suckers to get a grip on the surface beneath them so that they can move quickly. The suckers also come in handy when the leech wants to drink some blood. Each worm has both male and female parts. When a pair of them mate, they are fertilizing each other's eggs.

When a leech is firmly attached to another animal, it slices through the skin with its three sharp jaws. At the same time, it injects a painkilling chemical into the wound so that the victim feels nothing. Another chemical, hirudin, prevents the blood from clotting. Then the leech is free to suck up its meal.

Many different types of leeches are found in jungles, marshes, and other wetland areas around the world. They usually find their own food by attaching to the bodies of humans and animals that pass through their habitats. If you ever find a leech stuck to your skin, don't panic. They hardly ever carry any diseases. Just grab hold of it and pull. Their suckers are not strong enough to hold them on too tightly.

Bleeding the Patient

During the Middle Ages, leeches almost disappeared from some parts of the world. They were constantly being hunted so they could be used by doctors. Leeches seemed to be the solution to almost every problem. An overweight patient? Slap on a few leeches and he would lose some weight. A sick, tired patient? No problem. Slap on

A Giant Leech

The Amazon giant leech is 18 inches (45.7 cm) long and 3 inches (7.6 cm) wide. It can drain 0.14 ml of blood a minute. Two of these giants were found in the 1970s in a pond in French Guiana. Until then, they were thought to be extinct. None had been spotted since 1893. Scientists began breeding them in a laboratory in California. Within three years, they had 750 of them. They're especially interested in studying the powerful anticoagulant the Amazon giants produce.

A doctor placed this leech on a patient to suck up excess blood.

some more leeches. They would suck out all the "bad blood" that was causing the sickness. Soon, the patient would be as good as new. To speed up the cure, sometimes as many as fifty of the worms were set all over the patient's body.

The trouble was that "bad blood" does not cause diseases. The worst thing to do for a weakened patient is to remove blood. That just causes the person more weakness, and sometimes even death. When doctors discovered that germs caused diseases, they quit paying attention to leeches. For decades, the use of leeches to help patients was ridiculed by the medical profession.

Leeches Save an Ear

In recent years, however, the medical profession has been giving the worms a second look. In 1985, for instance, a dog in Medford, Massachusetts, attacked five-year-old Guy Condelli and bit off his right ear. Dr. Joseph Upton reattached the ear in a ten-hour operation. But right away there were problems. Before the veins inside could heal, they filled with blood and turned the ear purple. Once the blood was stuck in the veins, there was no way the veins could ever heal. It looked like young Guy would still lose his ear after all.

But then Dr. Upton had an idea. Why not use leeches to drain the excess blood? A company in Wales agreed to fly thirty "medicinal leeches" from London, England, to Massachusetts. Dr. Upton picked up the worms and used eight of them on the boy's ear. Immediately, they began sucking up the excess blood and allowed the ear to heal. A few days later, Guy went home with his ear intact. [1]

In 2004, the United States Food and Drug Administration approved the use of leeches as medical devices. It said that "surgeons have once again begun to use medicinal leeches as a means to restore venous blood circulation following cosmetic and reconstructive surgery." [2]

Leeches have already saved one little boy's ear. Maybe someday, they could save your life.

Chapter Notes

Chapter 1. Mosquitoes: Tiny Flying Terrors

1. Julia Laude, "Health Watch: The Best Way to Heal Mosquito Bites," webcenter11.com, June 28, 2017, http://www.webcenter11.com/tvtv/content/news/Health-Watch-The-Best-Way-To-Heal-Mosquito-Bites-431406133.html.

2. "Mosquito Traps," Mosquito World, 2018, http://www.mosquitoworld.net/mosquito-control/traps/.

3. Laura Riparbelli, "Stinky Feet, Scented Deodorants Attract Mosquitoes," ABC News, July 13, 2011, https://abcnews.go.com/Technology/stinky-feet-scented-deodorants-attract-mosquitoes/story?id=14065146.

Chapter 2. Vampire Bats: Preying on Sleeping Victims

1. "Vampire Bats," BatWorlds, November 5, 2013, http://www.batworlds.com/vampire-bat/.

Chapter 3. Head Lice: Making a Home in Your Hair

1. "How Long Does It Take for Nits (Lice Eggs) to Hatch?" Lice Doctors, accessed April 16, 2018, https://www.licedoctors.com/blog/how-long-does-it-take-for-lice-eggs-to-hatch.html.

2. Elea Carey, "A Close Look at Lice Bites," Heathline.com, accessed April 16, 2018, https://www.healthline.com/health/lice-bites.

Chapter 4. Lampreys: Lurking in the Rivers

1. "Sea Lamprey: A Great Lakes Invader," Great Lakes Fishery Commission, 2018, http://www.glfc.org/sea-lamprey.php.

2. University of Oklahoma, "Sea Lamprey Genome Mapped," ScienceDaily, February 28, 2013, https://www.sciencedaily.com/releases/2013/02/130228171510.htm.

Chapter 5. Fleas: Spreading Death and Disease

1. Anna van Nostrand, "Got the Plague? 10 Ways to Cure It (or at Least Try)," Dig Ventures, April 14, 2015, https://digventures.com/2015/04/got-the-plague-10-ways-to-cure-it-or-at-least-try/.

2. Carole Bos, "The Black Death—Biological Warfare," Awesome Stories, October 7, 2013, https://www.awesomestories.com/asset/view/The-Black-Death-Biological-Warfare.

3. Steve Sternberg, "The Plague," *Washington Post,* October 4, 1994, https://www.washingtonpost.com/archive/lifestyle/wellness/1994/10/04/the-plague/4342cc55-27de-4576-bce3-713a058ddd3c/?utm_term=.b437da7be086.

Chapter 6. Leeches: Performing Medical Miracles

1. Dr. W. Clifford Jones, "Is It Losing an Ear or Using Bloodsuckers?" Canada Free Press, March 19, 2006, http://canadafreepress.com/medical/surgery031906.htm.

2. Associated Press, "FDA Approves Leeches as Medical Devices," June 28, 2004, NBCNews.com, http://www.nbcnews.com/id/5319129/ns/health-health_care/t/fda-approves-leeches-medical-devices/#.Wo7ZscJ3tHh.

Glossary

anticoagulant A substance that prevents blood from coagulating, or thickening.

artery A blood vessel that carries blood away from the heart.

capillary The smallest blood vessel. Capillaries connect arteries to veins.

cartilage The flexible, whitish connective tissue found instead of bones in fish and human ears.

DDT An insecticide (dichloro-diphenyltrichloroethane) once used to kill mosquitoes.

draculin An anticoagulant found in the saliva of vampire bats.

echolocation The ability to locate objects by reflected sound.

hirudin An anticoagulant found in the saliva of leeches.

histamine A compound released as an allergic reaction to fight substances such as pollen or insect saliva.

immune Resistant to a particular infection or poison.

insecticide A chemical that kills insects.

louse A tiny insect that lives in human hair and feeds on blood.

malaria A sometimes fatal fever, often carried by mosquitoes in tropical regions.

nit A louse egg.

proboscis A tube used to suck nectar or blood into the mouth.

rabies An often fatal disease of the nervous system. The virus causing the disease is often transmitted through a bite.

regurgitate To throw up swallowed food.

repellant A substance that keeps insects away.

TFM A chemical lampricide, or lamprey killer.

vein A blood vessel that carries blood to the heart.

Further Reading

Books

Keiser, Cody. *Fleas*. New York, NY: PowerKids Press, 2015.

Kiepels, Alicia Z. *Vampires: The Truth Behind History's Creepiest Bloodsuckers*. North Mankato, MN: Capstone Press, 2015.

Marsico, Katie. *Leeches*. New York, NY: Scholastic, 2015.

Rake, Matthew. *Creatures of the Rain Forest*. Minneapolis, MN: Lerner Publishing Group, 2015.

Winters, Kari-Lynn, and Ishta Mercutio. *Bite into Bloodsuckers*. Markham, Ontario, Canada: Fitzhenry and Whiteside, 2015.

Websites

National Geographic Kids: Vampire Bats

kids.nationalgeographic.com/animals/vampire-bat/#yikes-vampirebat. png

Learn more about the vampire bat.

National Ocean Service: What Is a Sea Lamprey?

oceanservice.noaa.gov/facts/sea-lamprey.html

Read fascinating facts about the lamprey.

Teens Health: What Are Lice?

kidshealth.org/en/teens/head-lice.html

Get more information about lice and how to kill them or prevent an infestation.

Index